I've Changed My Mind

Change Your Thoughts to Transform Your Life

by Pastor Ron McKey

📖 Readable Reach

Edited by Readable Reach
Book Layout © 2017 BookDesignTemplates.com

I've Changed My Mind: Change Your Thoughts to Transform Your Life/ Pastor Ron McKey. -- 1st ed.

Print ISBN 978-1-7343301-0-6
Also available as an eBook

Introduction

This book comes as a result of seeing too many people suffer with anxiety, depression, and guilt. Sometimes, people cannot see a way out of that cycle, to the point that they choose to commit suicide. It is a tragedy that sadly is on the rise, particularly among men.

I've Changed My Mind: Change Your Thoughts to Transform Your Life is an attempt to help turn the tide. I want people to know that there is a very real source of hope, and there is a way out of their suffering. It is a renewal of the mind that can lead to abundant life.

This book addresses where negative (and sometimes lethal) thoughts come from, how to identify them, how to change those thought patterns, and where to focus instead, so you can grow in faith and joy.

These messages were originally delivered as sermons in the fall of 2019 in observance of Suicide Prevention and Awareness Month. My hope is that through these words, people will turn *away* from isolation, depression, and thoughts of suicide and turn *toward* community and the Word of God, which brings true help, peace and freedom.

CONTENTS

Chapter 1

Recognize Harmful Thoughts

I want to start by giving you what I call some "fast facts" or "fun facts" about the human brain. On average, the human brain weighs about three pounds, and about 60% of your brain is fat.[1] So, the next time somebody calls you a "fathead", you say, "That's sounds about right."

If you were to connect all of the vessels that run through the brain, they would extend to over 100,000 miles! Does that not blow your mind? How we ever got duped into the theory of evolution, I'll never know. When you look at the human body, how intricately, delicately and divinely designed it is, you have to know that if there is such an amazing creation, somewhere there is a creator.

The Bible says that we are fearfully and wonderfully made (Psalm 139:14). We are not accidents, and we didn't evolve. If you look at DNA and the design of the human body, you have to conclude that God invested in you, and you are here for a purpose.

God invested in you, and you are here for a purpose.

Scientists tell us that we have about 50,000 thoughts per day, and the majority of those thoughts are negative. That means that every morning when you wake up, it is going to be an uphill climb just to fight your way out of negativity and to stay positive.

To do so, you need the Word of God. You need a mind that is focused on God just to be able to get up and out of the pit. So many amazing things happen in our minds, and where you focus your mind will determine the direction of your life.

Something else that is significant is that your brain is an organ just like your heart, your lungs, your liver, your kidneys, and every other organ in your body. But something different about the brain is, when someone has a mental illness, there is a huge stigma attached to it. But, it shouldn't be that way.

When someone has a heart attack, and the heart is not firing just right or functioning like it should, we don't label that person and put a stigma on him, saying, "You know what? I always knew there was something weird about him. I don't want to hang out with him anymore." We do the opposite! We go *to* him and encourage him.

When somebody has to have surgery to get an organ fixed, repaired, or removed, we don't put a stigma on that person and say, "You know, I always knew something wasn't right." Again, we do the opposite, and we go *to* him or her and embrace that person. I am just saying that mental illness should not have a stigma attached to it like it does, because the brain is an organ just like your other organs.

Everyone is Dealing with Something

I believe God can help us to overcome putting stigmas on people, because the truth of the matter is, every one of us is dealing with something. Every one of us has a battle going on in our head; we are all facing something. So, you are not alone.

If you are one of those people who says, "Well, not me. I've got it all together," let me say this: You are dealing with *two* things — denial and lying. So, we're going to go ahead and move you to the front of the list of people who need help. Every one of us needs help.

Church should never be a place where we all come in and everybody thinks everybody is perfect, because we are not. Church isn't about coming together and being perfect. Church is about coming together, even when we are broken and *don't* have it all together. It is a hospital where we can get better.

Recently, a young pastor named Jarrid Wilson from Harvest Church in California (Greg Laurie's church) committed suicide. He had battled depression and the things he had gone through in the past, to the point where he said, "I even feel like it's my ministry to help lead others out of depression." He was an author and had blogged and vlogged extensively on suicide and overcoming. He lost that battle, and he took his own life, leaving behind his wife and two small children.[2]

I want you to know that nobody is immune to this battle that goes on in the mind. Nobody is immune to these thoughts of suicide, and I am hopeful that this book will help us talk about the issue and not leave it covered up or ignored. There is help, and we can get better. I want us to understand just how important it is.

Over one million people worldwide this year will commit suicide. 40,000 people in the United States alone will take their own lives, and the majority will be men. The number one killer of young people between the ages of 15 to 24 is suicide. That means that if you have a teenager or young adult at home, there is a risk of your child dying by his or her own hands.

We have to bring this out, even in church, and begin to open the door to let people know that they can get help, and we can help them. We can point them in the right direction and connect them with organizations. If you are suffering with anything, let somebody know. Let your church know. We want to help you get through whatever it is that you are going through.

Even the Bible speaks about this issue. In fact, there is an entire book in the Bible called Lamentations that deals with depression, written by one of God's prophets, Jeremiah. Jeremiah was a major prophet. He was one of those guys whom God tremendously used, and yet, the entire book of Lamentations is dealing with his failures. Let's look at one of these verses. This is Lamentations chapter three.

Lamentations 3:17-19

I have been deprived of peace. I have forgotten what prosperity is. I have forgotten what it's like to even be happy anymore. And so I say my splendor is gone and all that I had hoped for from the Lord. I remember my affliction and my wandering, the bitterness and the gall.

He is dealing with depression. The word *prosperity* there isn't a dollar sign; it doesn't mean finances. It means quality of life. When you are prosperous, it means you are happy and blessed, and you have a good quality of life. He is saying he has forgotten what it looks like to be happy; he has forgotten what a good life looks like or sounds like.

When he says, "I remember…", he is focusing on all of the bad things in his life. He is pushing himself down deeper and deeper into a well of despair, remembering and focusing on everything that has gone wrong.

All of us have done that, right? All of us have looked at the negative things in our lives and focused just on the stupid things that we have said or done. Then, we build those things up in our minds.

Jeremiah is dealing with that. He is in this place, this frame of mind, where all he can see are the terrible things that are happening in his life. He is going through depression and struggling.

Causes of Depression and Suicide

There may be many causes of depression, which can lead to suicide, but I want to give you two causes. They are often linked together, and these are markers that we need to be aware of. One of them is faulty thinking.

If you think wrong, you will believe wrong.

Faulty thinking is just like what Jeremiah was doing in Lamentations. It is when we begin to build scenarios up in our minds, and make things up, saying things like, "Everybody is thinking *this* about me. This guy over here doesn't like me. My boss feels this way about me..."

That is faulty thinking, and it does not lead to anything that is going to help you. That faulty thinking just keeps you in a place of depression, and we have got to move beyond that. We have to take control of our thoughts.

The second thing that often leads us down that road of depression is isolation. Here's the thing about the enemy: He loves to isolate us. The enemy loves to make you feel like you are the only person going through anything and that you are the only person who is struggling.

The truth of the matter is, if we would just come out and say, "Hey, here's what I'm facing," chances are, there are a lot of people who would say, "Yeah, me too! I thought I was the only one."

We know that is not true and that we *all* deal with things in our lives, but the enemy wants to separate us and get us to think that we are the only ones. Listen to this powerful statement:

> *If the only voice you are listening to is your voice, you are in trouble.*

If the only person speaking into your life is yourself, you are already in trouble, and you need to get some other people from the outside speaking life into you. It's just that simple. That is one of the major reasons behind churches having small groups.

It is in small groups that people begin to share about family, kids, marriage, themselves, their struggles, their victories... and maybe there are a lot of people who are going through what you are going through, and they can speak into your life and help you. So, I encourage you, if you have not gotten involved with a group, it is not too late.

Renewing Your Mind

Let's look at several Scripture verses about the mind. These are foundational Scriptures, and the first one is in the book of Romans. This is one of my favorite verses, and it is a powerful, fundamental verse. It talks about how we begin this journey of renewing our mind.

Romans 12:2

Do not conform to the pattern of this world, but be transformed by the renewing of your mind. Then you will be able to test and approve what God's will is—His good, pleasing and perfect will.

The first thing that Paul says through the Holy Spirit is, "Do not conform to the pattern of this world." What he is saying is, do not fit the mold of the world. The world wants to mold you to be a certain way. It doesn't want you to be *this* way; it wants you to be *that* way. The first thing that God is saying is, don't conform to worldly standards.

We are *in* the world, the Bible says, but we are not *of* the world (John 15:19). And while we are in this world, we are not supposed to act like the world, talk like the world, or behave like the world. We have dual citizenship.

Not only do we belong here on Earth, but we have a home in Heaven. God says, "I want you to focus on that. I want you to establish the Kingdom of Heaven." So, do not conform to the pattern of this world; do not let the world fit you into its mold.

Instead, be transformed. We are supposed to be different. When you are born again, you begin this journey of transformation. God does not expect perfection, but He does expect transformation. You are on a journey to becoming something different. The way that happens is by the renewing of your mind. In this book, we are going to talk about how to do that.

When you are born again, God does a work inside of you, but He doesn't change your thinking. It is *our* responsibility to change how we think and begin to go in a different way. Recently, I had this realization:

A renewed mind comes through repentance.

Often, when we use the word repentance, we connect it with something negative, like "I got caught, and now I have to say I'm sorry." That's not what repentance is. First of all, there is nothing negative about repentance. Everything about it is positive. Everything about repentance is a privilege, and we get the opportunity to correct things we've gotten wrong. Repentance means to do a 180.

But when it comes to renewing your mind, let me show you why we need to understand what repentance really is. It comes from the Greek word *metanoia*, and that word is made up of two separate words: the word *meta*, meaning change, and the word *noia*, meaning mind.

So, to repent does not mean to say, "I'm sorry I got caught." Repent means, "I'm going to change my mind [hence the title of this book], and what I was doing, I choose to no longer do. I've made a choice that I'm not going to go *that* way. I'm going to go *this* way." It is a powerful thing that we have to begin to understand.

Have you ever had a crazy thought, even in church? Maybe you were sitting in church, and somewhere from way out in left field, this thought comes, and you are thinking, *where did that come from?* It may be a bad thought, a wrong thought, a perverse thought, or just a wicked thought. It makes you think, *what is going on? I am in church. Where did this come from?*

I think we have all done that. So the question is, how can we stop that from happening? I've done some research on this, and the very best theological answer that I can give you on how to keep those thoughts from coming is this: You can't. There is no way to avoid it. It is going to happen.

What we have to learn to do when those thoughts come, is to manage them or learn how to repent, change our minds, or change the channel.

Change the Channel

I have a remote control, and I have a special relationship with the remote, because when I was a kid growing up, I *was* the remote control. We had three channels (well, there were four, but nobody watched PBS), and whenever dad said, "Change the channel," the remote control (me) got up and clicked it to another one. So, I can relate to the remote.

But, if you are ever watching a show or program and something with a cringe factor comes on, you do not have to sit through it. You probably have a remote that you can use to change the channel.

Maybe you don't like the content. Maybe you don't like the people. Maybe you don't like the drama. Whatever it is, you don't have to sit there and force yourself to watch it. In Philippians chapter four, Paul says:

Philippians 4:8

Finally, brethren, whatsoever things are true, whatsoever things are honest, whatsoever things are just, whatsoever things are pure, whatsoever things are lovely, whatsoever things are of good report; if there be any virtue, and if there be any praise, think on these things.

That is where our minds are supposed to go. Think about how this verse would change your life if you really put it into play. What if everything we did had to run through this filter? I'm telling you, it would make your life and your mental health a whole lot better.

Can you imagine getting a phone call, and you say, "Before we begin this conversation, can I ask you something? What you are about to say, is it true? Is it honest? Is it just? Is that pure? Hello?... Hello?…"

Before we watch a program, we should ask ourselves, is this something that is going to lift me or take me down? In other words, you need to make a filter in your life. Whatever things are true, honest, just or pure, *those* are the things that we want to spend our time dwelling on.

You might have something come into your life like fear. Nobody likes to live in fear, yet we live in a pretty frightening world. There are a lot of things happening around us. There are a lot of bad people. There are a lot of things that could go wrong, but you don't want to stay there dwelling on those things.

I'm not trying to oversimplify this, but I'm also not trying to complicate it. You don't want to live in fear. You need to think from a place of comfort. You need to start thinking, *when I am fearful, what is the steadfast thing? What is the one thing in my life that does not change?* That is Jesus Christ.

When I am fearful, I will go to that place of comfort and say, "I do live in a fearful world; there are a lot of bad things that happen. But, I've got a Savior, who is Jesus, and I can trust Him. I believe that God is going to get me through this."

You have to change the channel in order to keep strong in your mind. When you begin to worry and it feels like life is coming at you at an unreal pace, when you can't keep up and you are picturing all of the things that could go wrong, you can't stay there.

You need to mentally, on purpose, change the channel and go from worry to saying, "I am going to live a life of hope."

I would much rather live with hope than dread. I would much rather live in a world that says, "Things are going to work out; they are going to turn out for me." I'm going to be that person who is filled with hope, rather than the one always saying, "There is no way this is going to work out for me."

Have you ever found that what you spend a lot of time worrying about never happens? We waste a lot of time and energy worrying about what *might* happen, but I think we would be better off if we put that energy into saying, "My God is a God of hope, and I am going to trust Him." Remember what the Psalmist said: "This is the day the Lord has made. I will rejoice and be glad in it (Psalm 118:24)."

You can make the choice to rejoice.

Often, we have chaos and toxic stuff in our minds. We constantly have negative thoughts and images. However, you can't dwell there. You have got to change the channel. You need to go to a place of peace, and I'll tell you, there is no better place where you can find peace than in God's Word.

There is no better way you can have your heart comforted or your spirit lifted than when you begin to get a Scripture or a Word from God for your life. It is without a doubt, life changing.

Defeating Strongholds

When you see something, and that cringe factor happens, you need to say, "I'm not staying here. I'm not thinking *this* way; I'm going to think *that* way." But sometimes, when you try to change the channel, it won't change! A thought that won't change is a stronghold.

A stronghold is a fortified place where the enemy hides and embeds himself so that it is very difficult, if not impossible, to extract him. We have strongholds in our minds, of thoughts and addictions that the enemy hides in, and it is very difficult to find freedom. Let me give you a verse that might help in these situations. It is from 2 Corinthians 10:

2 Corinthians 10:4

The weapons we fight with are not the weapons of the world. On the contrary, they have divine power to demolish strongholds. We demolish arguments and every pretension that sets itself up against the knowledge of God, and we take captive every thought to make it obedient to Christ.

Understand that there is a battle being waged for your mind, a battle that is going on in your head. What Paul is saying here is that the weapons we fight with are not the weapons of the world. We have a spiritual arsenal that God has given us to overcome the enemy.

Now, the interesting thing about this verse is that this is a reference to the walls of Jericho. Do you remember the story of

Joshua and the walls of Jericho from Joshua chapter 6? Think about how the weapons of our warfare are not carnal; they are spiritual. But, the Bible says they are mighty through God.

Think about the scenario of Jericho and the army of Israel. Here is how they fought the battle: They just walked around the walls. That's foolish! There's no power in that! But there was in this case.

Can you imagine the people from Jericho watching what God's army did? They were blowing horns, or shofars, and they were yelling. I'm sure the people of Jericho were behind the wall mockingly saying, "Woo. That's pretty scary."

But that was about the time that the walls began to crumble. On their own, the trumpets and yelling were foolishness, but when God anointed and used them, they became powerful tools of deliverance.

I don't understand *how* prayer works, but I know *that* it works. I don't have to fully understand it to believe in it, act on it, and have it operate in my life. Just speaking words into a room, how does that change things? Well, it doesn't in itself, but in God, it becomes powerful.

Songs are powerful. A worship service is not just singing. How can that change my life? Well, when God anoints it, it becomes life changing.

The Bible says that God will even use the foolishness of preaching. He'll take some guy giving you a 30-minute message, anoint that, take something out of the message, apply it to your heart, and you can walk away saying, "Man! I got a Word from God! God spoke to me!"

So, every weapon that we have, on its own, doesn't make sense, but because they are spiritual and God anoints them, they become powerful. Our prayers are powerful. Our worship is powerful. A Word from God is powerful. All of these things are weapons that we use to overcome the enemy.

This is the definition of a mental stronghold: It is a lie that Satan whispers into your mind as a thought that then grows to become a giant that controls your life. I think it's pretty accurate that what starts out as a small thought can end up becoming a giant in our lives.

Do you realize that your life will always go in the direction of your strongest thought? Whatever you are thinking on the most, is the direction your life is going to go. Satan loves to plant seeds and then turn molehills into mountains, so they become strongholds.

David vs. Goliath

Let me give an example of how we can battle this and come against strongholds in our minds. I'm going to go to the story of David and Goliath from 1 Samuel 17. Who doesn't love that story? There was this giant, Goliath, who stopped the army of Israel, and every day, he would stand in front of them, becoming a stronghold.

He said, "There is no way you are going to go forward. There is no way you are going to get around me. I am going to control you." And for a length of time, he stopped Israel in its tracks. They couldn't go forward. They couldn't have victory. They couldn't do anything but just sit there, camped out in their tents, depressed because they couldn't go on doing what God wanted them to do.

The same things that David did are the things we can do in order to have victory in our lives. Here is what David knew: There was no way he could reason with Goliath. Goliath was unreasonable. He was the biggest, baddest dude in the room. There was no way he was going to reason with him and convince him he needed to change. And David knew for sure that he could not ignore a 10-foot giant that stood in his way.

The same is true with the problems *you* face. You cannot argue with strongholds. You cannot deny that they exist. You have to deal with them. What did David do? The first thing he did was run toward the giant. He acknowledged there was a giant that needed to be tackled. He thought, *I can't ignore this; I've got to face the giant in my life.*

Maybe one of the greatest breakthroughs that you'll have today is that you come to a place of saying, "You know what? I've got to face the giant in my life. I've got to face the addiction. I've got to face the problem. I've got to face the stronghold and admit that I've got something going on that needs to be dealt with." That is the first step in overcoming and living in greater victory.

You've got a face the giant.

The second thing that David did was, he spoke God's Word. Now, I know that may be old school, and you may have never heard that before, but David looked at Goliath and said what

God said. He began to say that Goliath was going to fall. He said, "You come to me with a sword and a spear, but I come to you in the name of the Lord, our God (1 Samuel 17:45)."

There are some situations in life where you need to begin to say what God says about your life. You need to say, "I am more than a conqueror through Jesus Christ (Romans 8:37)," or, "I can do all things through Christ who strengthens me (Philippians 4:13)." You need to begin to say, "Whom the Son sets free is free indeed (John 8:36)." Agree with what the Word says.

Jesus did that when he fought Satan in the desert and had that incredible spiritual battle. Every time Satan tempted Him, Jesus responded by saying, "Here is what the Word of God says…" There is no greater way to overcome temptation than to say what God says about your situation.

The third thing that David did was, he trusted in God's covenant. He knew he had a covenant he could count on, because when God makes a promise, He never breaks it.

Three Steps for Renewing Your Thinking

I am trying to give you ground to stand on and show you how to fight that spiritual battle. I want to give you three steps for renewing your thinking after you have identified negative, harmful thoughts and begin to fight against them.

Resurrection

There is a thing called *resurrection power*, which is to realize that you have been raised to a new life. That is what it means to be born again.

If you have been born again, you need to say to yourself, "I have been raised to life, and I need to live with that mindset. I am going to live like a new creation in Christ. I understand that what God has done on the inside of me is going to work its way to the outside of me. Because Jesus rose from the dead, I am promised victory."

That is good news! You can face your problems knowing that Jesus, through His power, has already overcome that problem.

Rejoice

This is simple. Yet, because it is so simple, we miss it. If I want to renew my mind, I have to make the choice to rejoice. You can choose joy. Did you know you can choose to be happy? In the Bible, Paul says, "Rejoice in the Lord always, and again I say, rejoice (Philippians 4:4)."

We do not have to choose worry; we can choose joy. We do not have to choose chaos; we can choose joy. We do not have to choose all the drama; we can choose joy.

We have to make the choice to rejoice and make it a lifestyle. You may not feel like it. We've all been there. But, we are going to go ahead and rejoice anyway, because we are rejoicing in the Lord.

Remember

I encourage you to take a moment and remember how good God has been to you. Some of you are not supposed to be here because Satan told you he was going to kill you. But here you are, still going. Some of you are still overcoming. Satan said "You are going to die from this," but you are still alive.

Remember all of the good things that God has done for you. Look back on your life and say, "There were times when I failed God, but He has never failed me."

Remembering how good God has been lifts me up out of depression. Remembering how good God is lets me know that He is the same yesterday, today, and forever. Whatever I am facing, I have a God I can trust to walk me through.

In this chapter, we talked about recognizing the thoughts we have that need to change and how to face strongholds. Then, we began the topic of renewing the mind. In the next chapter, we will look more at the idea of filtering your thoughts, learn a technique for replacing harmful thoughts with biblical ones, and look at how having a pastor along the way can help.

ACTION STEPS

1) Find a small group in a local church to get connected with.

2) Practice identifying negative thoughts and "changing the channel" to confidence in Jesus and God's Word.

Filter and Replace

I magine you have a couple of baskets, each filled with food. One basket has junk food in it, and the other has a better choice of food (health food). Since both baskets are filled with food, they are similar, yet they are also different.

Here is the thing about junk food: It's everywhere. It's easily and readily accessible. You don't have to hunt it down and find it; it's usually right there in your face. There is a fast food restaurant on every corner. Junk food is at every cash register. Even at the register in a hardware store, there is junk food, soda, etc.. It's always right there, and it's usually cheap and fast.

The difference between that and the healthier basket is, sometimes the healthier choice is not always the easier choice. In fact, if you are going to eat healthy, one of the things you are going to find out is that you have to be intentional. You have to plan ahead, make decisions beforehand, and prepare. And it's not fast.

If you are going to have a good meal, you usually have to go into a restaurant (not a fast food restaurant), sit down, order, and wait for it to be prepared and brought to you. So, it takes a little bit more time and effort... and it costs you more.

What we are really talking about is our thoughts. It's true with food that you are what you eat, and if you make good choices, if you choose the better or healthier options, you are going to feel better physically, and you are also going to feel better about yourself. You are going to like the person in the mirror more.

The same is true with the way we think. Our thinking is either going to elevate us and help us, or it's going to drag us down. There is a Scripture verse that talks about this. Proverbs 23:7 says, "For as he thinks in his heart, so is he."

Whatever you spend time thinking about, that's what you are going to become.

In fact, this is a true statement for every one of us. You are today where you are because of what you thought about yesterday, last week, or last month. Our thoughts direct us and drive us. Our thoughts position us. Your thoughts control your life, and your life is always going to move in the direction of your strongest thought.

So, we are where we are in life, because of something that we thought about beforehand. Keep that in mind. Read this statement: If you do not think it, you will not do it.

This is because everything we do first originates as a thought. Now, that could be good or bad. For every good thing you do, you think about it first and then do it. For every bad thing you do, you think about it first, and then you do it.

Have a Filter

Let's look at a couple of verses that we have already seen and approach them from a slightly different angle.

Philippians 4:8

Finally, brethren, whatsoever things are true, whatsoever things are honest, whatsoever things are just, whatsoever things are pure, whatsoever things are lovely, whatsoever things are of good report; if there be any virtue, and if there be any praise, think on these things.

We could also say, "Think on these things". We are going to take this Word, meditate on it, and break it down. Paul is teaching us, "Listen, these are the things in life that you need to put your focus toward." In other words, Philippians 4:8 is the mental filter for your life.

One of my responsibilities at home is that every couple of months, I am in charge of changing the air filters. I have to get up in the ceiling and pull those things down, because if I don't change the air filters, my house will not stay cool. My air conditioning unit will be working overtime, meaning it is going to wear out quickly. So, it takes a little bit of effort.

I don't usually think about it, but when I hold up the new filter, take out the old filter, and put them side-by-side, there is a huge difference between the old and the new. I do not realize how much dirt circulates through my filters until I put the two next to each other.

When you take Philippians 4:8 and filter your thoughts through this verse, it is going to take out some of those impurities. It is going to take out some of those things that are holding you back and affecting you in a negative way.

The filter that we see life through shapes us. If we take everything in life and run it through this filter (whatever things are true, honest, just, pure, lovely, or of good report), and then think on these things, life automatically gets better, because we are what we think about.

Now, that word *meditate* at the end of this verse is not some New Age thing. That is something that has been around for a long, long time. In fact, meditation comes from the Bible. It is a God thing, and all that it means is that we are to sit down and focus on something.

It has different meanings when you look it up in the Greek. It could mean "to ponder". That means there are times in life when you just need to hit the pause button, sit down, think about life, look at where you are, and reflect. So, it could mean "to ponder or reflect", but it also means "to declare". I am supposed to *say* something.

I've got a great devotion book that I love, and it's how I start my day before I get into my Bible. Part of it is reading a Scripture passage and breaking the Word down, and part of it is a prayer that is written out. The last part is a declaration.

I am the first one up. I get up at 4:30 every morning, and no one is around. I speak the verse for that day, and when I get to the declaration, I speak it out loud, because I want to hear myself saying what God says. I speak this declaration over my life. It's just a great way to start your day, to speak God's Word over your life and into your life.

The next verse for us to look at is in Isaiah chapter 55:

Isaiah 55:8-9

"For my thoughts are not your thoughts, neither are your ways my ways,"declares the Lord."As the heavens are higher than the earth, so are my ways higher than your ways and my thoughts than your thoughts."

I cannot read this without making this comment: "Praise God! I am so glad God does not think like me." Here is what He is saying: "I don't just think at a little bit higher level than you. Imagine how far the heavens are above the earth. Those are my thoughts."

That tells me right away that I want to think *God's* thoughts. I want to think like God, because He's got a much better way of thinking.

I know just from reading that passage that I cannot go wrong if I do life God's way, run life through God's filter, and do what it is that God has called me to do. You cannot go to the next level in life thinking the same old, worn-out thoughts that you have been thinking for the last 20 years. You can't go to another level in life without getting your thoughts closer to God's thoughts.

Repent and Replace

Let's look again at the word *repent*. As I mentioned in Chapter One, often when we hear the word repent, we think of it with a negative connotation, but the word not only means to do a 180; the literal meaning is "to change your mind", to change the way you are thinking.

Why? Because you cannot change your life until you change your thinking, which brings me to a principle from the Word of God that I call "repent and replace". Let me give an example of what I'm talking about.

If I ever have the thought that I am a failure, the first thing I need to do when I begin to dwell on that thought or experience that emotion is to repent from that and say, "God, I'm sorry for thinking that. I apologize for having that poor self-image. I apologize to you for thinking so little of your creation, and I ask you to forgive me."

I am going to replace that thought with another one. I'm going to change it and begin to think that I am worth something. I am not going to think I'm a failure; I am going to begin to say that a good man falls seven times, but he keeps getting up (Proverbs 24:16). He may fall seven times, but he gets up eight. I'm not a failure. I am down, but not out.

When I look at something in life and have the thought, *that's impossible*, I'm going to repent and say, "God, I apologize for that kind of thinking. I apologize for looking at my situation through my eyes and not your eyes. Through my eyes, it is impossible, but with you, God, nothing is impossible."

If I am ever in a place where I want to give up and say, "God, you know I can't do this," I need to repent of that and say, "God, I can do all things through Christ who strengthens me (Philippians 4:13)."

And if I say that I can't or God won't, or I'm afraid, I need to repent and say, "God, forgive me for being fearful, because you have not given me a spirit of fear. You have given me a spirit of love and power and of sound mind (2 Timothy 1:7)."

Norman Vincent Peale, who was a motivational speaker and author who died many years ago, told a story about when he was in Hong Kong on vacation. He was just walking around the city, enjoying all the sights, sounds, and foods that the city had to offer, and as he was walking along, he came to a tattoo shop.

In the window were many examples of different tattoos you could get, but one of them caught his attention. Right in the window, right up front, in big, bold letters, was a tattoo that said, "Born to Lose".

Norman Peale said, "I couldn't just walk away; I had to go in." So, he went in and asked the shop owner about that tattoo in the front window. He asked, "Does anyone ever really get that tattoo? The owner replied, "Yes," and then in broken English, he said, "Before they tattoo it on the arm, they first have tattooed it on the mind." 3

Isn't that true? What we get in our minds and what we focus on, pretty soon becomes where we go and what we begin to believe about ourselves.

God's Word is True

This next verse is significant, as well: Romans 3:4. I want to focus on the first part of the verse. "Certainly not, indeed. Let God be true and every human being a liar."

That's good advice. Let God be true. Let whatever God is saying be the truth, and let every man, every other opinion and influence, be a liar. In other words, choose to believe God's Word above anyone else's word, and don't worry about who the person is. I have made the decision to let my life be governed by the Word of God.

Why? -because His ways are higher than my ways, and His thoughts are higher than my thoughts. I am going to believe God first, and whatever man has to say is not going to trump the Word of God. In Genesis 3, Adam and Eve are in the Garden, and the Bible says:

Genesis 3:1

Now the serpent was more crafty than any of the wild animals the LORD God had made. He said to the woman, "Did God really say, 'You must not eat from any tree in the garden?'"

The serpent is Satan, and God had just given the command to Adam and Eve, "You need to watch over the Garden. Do not eat from the tree of the knowledge of good and evil." Satan shows up and says, "Did God really say you must not eat from the tree?" Those four words (did God really say) are going to challenge your faith more than any other words in the English language. More than any words you will ever hear are those four words.

From the beginning of time until now, Satan has not changed his approach. In everything you go through in life, Satan is always going to ask that question. "Are you sure that is what God said? Are you sure that is what God's Word says? Are you sure that is what God meant?" Until you settle that answer in your heart and decide, "Let God be true and every man be a liar," you are always going to struggle spiritually.

That has always been Satan's approach. In fact, if you read through the Bible, this is what Jesus taught: Every trial, every storm, every temptation, every struggle that you face, comes for one reason.

Once you realize this, you will be more effective in life. Every struggle, every trial, everything that comes into your life is to get you to doubt God's Word.

That is always the goal of the enemy. That is always the breaking point. So, you are always going to deal with thoughts like, *is that what God is saying? Is that what God meant? Did God really say that? Well, that's probably not what God meant. I know what the Bible says, but it probably shouldn't be taken literally.*

You have to make the decision in your life to trust God's Word.

Everybody Needs a Pastor

Let me share something from my heart. I recently attended the funeral of *my* pastor, and I was so surprised by the effect it had on my life; I was a mess. For over 40 years, Dr. Dan Beller had been my pastor, and when I moved off to Bible school when I was a teenager, I knew that I needed to find a church I could get plugged into and get involved in.

I had a couple of options. One was a small church not far from where I lived. I immediately wanted to go to that church because I had come from a small church, and this was comfortable; it fit. However, I know God is not always interested in how comfortable I am.

I had already had a conversation with the pastor. He was going to give me some responsibilities and even pay me a little bit to work with the young people there. It wasn't much, but when you are in Bible school, let me tell you; every penny counts. So I said, "Man! This is what I want to do!" But, I had promised my aunt that I would not choose a church until I had visited her church.

So I thought, *I'll go to her church. Then I'll come back, and we'll get this party started.* The next week, I went to her 2000-member church and was intimidated and out of my league; I was fearful. But I sat there, and in that morning worship service, my pastor, Dr. Dan Beller, walked out on stage and began to teach and preach. In that moment, I literally heard the voice of God speak to my spirit, and He said, "This is your pastor, and this is your church."

I went back to the other pastor and had the conversations that I needed to have to set everything right. Then, I got involved in this new church. After I was there for a little while, God spoke to my heart again. He said, "I want you to place this man on a pedestal in your life. Not above me and not above my Word, but

I want you to elevate him to a position of honor in your life. I want you to place him on a pedestal."

For 40 years, he was my pastor. I cannot tell you how much I loved and cared for that man and appreciate his ministry.

A number of years ago, on a Tuesday morning around 10:00am (that is when we have our staff meetings), my wife came to my office, stuck her head in, and said, "Staff makes time for staff meetings. Are you coming?" I said, "No."

There were about a dozen people sitting around the table. We had staff reports, calendars, financials… All of these things were going on, and we had things that we needed to figure out. My wife said, "What do you mean, no?"
I said, "No, I'm not coming, because I'm done."

This was because I was going through what I called a perfect storm. There were church pressures, financial pressures, issues and problems, and on top of all of that, a good friend of mine had just died way too early in life.

My wife said, "What do you mean you're not coming? What do you mean you're done?"
I said, "I don't want to do this anymore. I'm through. It's over."
She said, "I don't know what that means."
I said, "I'm not sure either, but I have to leave. I just have to go. I'm not running away; I just need to drive. I'll call you in about an hour. I've just got to get my head together."

So, I drove and drove through a lot of places. It took me about 20 minutes to get through anger, but I got there. I drove a little bit longer through confusion and frustration, and finally, I came to the place where God wanted me, a little place on the side of the road called Help.

I picked up my phone, and I called my pastor. I remember what he said. "Hey Buddy! What's going on?" I said, "I need you, Pastor. I'm done. I quit."
He said, "Well, come talk to me."

So, I made an appointment, and we went to lunch. He listened, and then he said these words: "You don't want to quit."
I said, "Yeah, I'm pretty sure I do."

He said, "I'm pretty sure you don't, and let me tell you why. Here's what you are going to do: You are going to go back, and you are going to be better than you have ever been. Here's what you've learned that you *thought* you knew, but you didn't. You thought you were leaning on God, but you weren't. So, you are going to go back and do ministry, and this time, you are going to rely on God more and less on you. You are going to finish strong."

No one is immune to feelings or emotions, and there are times we need to ask for help in sorting through those emotions.

I told you that story to tell you that when God said, "I want you to put that man on a pedestal," it wasn't that he was perfect (although he was the most Christ-like man I've ever known). I didn't understand at the time, but after years went by, I began to realize why God said that.

He said, "If you don't put him on a pedestal, there will come a time when you will dishonor him, and when you dishonor him, you will dishonor the vessel that I am delivering the Word to you through. If you dishonor him, you will begin to devalue the Word that I have for you, because I am going to use him to bring the Word."

For 40 years of my life, he sat on a pedestal and spoke into my life. There are a couple of times he corrected me, but he always encouraged me. Everybody needs a pastor, and you need to come to the place where you honor the Word of God and put it in that place where you say, "God, your Word comes first." I encourage you to find that person in your life. Find that pastor through whom you will let God speak to you.

How Your Life Will Change

This next verse is significant. We talked about it in the first chapter. Remember in Romans 12:2, Paul writes:

Romans 12:2

Do not conform to the pattern of this world, but be transformed by the renewing of your mind. Then you will be able to test and approve what God's will is--His good, pleasing and perfect will.

Do not let the world mold you or shape you. Do not think like the world. Rather, be *transformed*. How do you transform? How do you change? The only way to change once Christ comes into your life is by the renewing of your mind.

When you are born again, God changes you from the inside out, but it is *your* responsibility to change your thinking. God says,

"This is on you. I am going to do the spiritual aspect of this, but the rest is up to you." Let me give you four areas or your life that, when you have renewed your mind, will change.

Actions

When you begin to renew your mind through the Word of God, your actions are going to line up. You will make better decisions, and by making better decisions, you will make fewer mistakes. When you renew your mind through the Word of God, you are going to learn to do the wise thing, not what you feel like or what others are doing. You will begin to do what Jesus would do.

I know this is old school, but it really is good: What would Jesus do? If you begin to frame your life around that phrase (What would Jesus do? What would He say? How would He respond?), you are going to see your life improve, because you will be living a life that is Christ-like. You are going to act differently, be wiser, make better decisions, and chart a better course for your life.

Love

With a renewed mind, you will begin to love unconditionally and not be so judgmental. You are not going to hold people to you standard or a false standard. You will begin to love them right where they are. That is without a doubt, a Christ thing.

You are also going to become more patient. Some of us could use that, right? We will be more kind and forgiving, because that is what the Bible tells us we need to be.

Speech

A renewed mind will also show up in your speech. Paul made this statement:

1 Corinthians 13:11

When I was a child, I talked like a child, I thought like a child, I reasoned like a child. When I became a man, I put away childish things.

This means that you are grown and not thinking or speaking childishly anymore. One of the number one problems in the church is not just the enemy, not Satan; it is spiritually immaturity. It is people who will not grow up and who remain spiritually childish.

Emotions

Last, it will show up in your emotions. Would you like to get off of that emotional roller coaster? The way to do it is to repeat what God says, and it will begin to work out in every area of your life. In Chapter Four, we will dive much deeper into the topic of controlling our emotions, but I wanted to touch on them here.

Two Pieces of Advice

I'll give my last two words of advice for this chapter. One is, don't believe everything you think. I'll give you a great example from the Word of God in the Old Testament.

There was a guy by the name of Naaman. He was a very important military leader, but he had this disease called leprosy, and
there was no cure. He had heard that there was a prophet in the
land whom God used to do miracles. So, he made the decision,
"I'm going to go see the prophet and see if he can do anything
for me."

He goes there with an entourage, his military brass, and they
come to the prophet's town. Elisha, the prophet, sends out his
servant, Gehazi. Elisha doesn't even come out himself! The servant comes and asks, "What is it that you need?" Naaman tells
him, and he goes back in to tell Elisha. When Gehazi comes out
again, he says, "My master sent me out to tell you, if you go
jump in the Jordan River not once, but seven times, you will be
healed."

That was a little bit offensive. Not only did the prophet not come
out, but he told this very important person to go jump in the river seven times! Naaman was so offended, he turned around and
started to leave.

He was convinced to go back, and here's what he said: "I
thought that the man of God would come out and pray some
kind of prayer over me, but he didn't even come out. He sent his
servant!"

That phrase "I thought" almost cost him his future and his healing. If you read the story, he dipped seven times in the Jordan
River. The seventh time, he came up cleansed from leprosy. But,
if he had followed the road that said, "Here's what I thought God
was going to do. Here's how I think God should operate. Here's
how I think this ought to play out...," he would not have been

healed. Sometimes we just need to trust God. Sometimes we just need to obey His Word.

Don't believe everything you think. Choose to believe God's Word.

The second piece of advice is, guard your mind from garbage. I first started in ministry as a children's pastor. One of the lessons I would teach was to bring garbage cans in and say, "Hey kids, listen. These are not garbage cans; these are your ears. If somebody comes trying to fill your head with garbage, just say, 'Stop! This is not a dump. I don't want to hear this.'"

Have you ever had a conversation in which someone just threw up on you verbally? "Everything is bad. Everything is negative. Everything is horrible…" It's like, "Man! I just want to shower because you've just thrown up on me for 30 minutes. I want to get out of here!"

You know what I'm talking about. Guard your mind from garbage in what you hear and what you read. Remember that it needs to go through a filter, because here's the thing: God wants you to have good mental health. God wants our minds to be renewed. God wants you to have your head together. God wants you to be able to think clearly, because that shapes the trajectory of your future.

To review, in this chapter, we talked again about having a filter for your thoughts, using a "repent and replace" method to replace negative thoughts with God-honoring thoughts, how important it is to find a good pastor, and the importance of trusting God's Word.

In the next chapter, we will discuss what it looks like to walk by faith, where thoughts come from in the first place, and the power of your will.

ACTION STEPS

1) **If you don't have one, find a good pastor who is more than just a preacher to you.**

2) **Repent of thinking you are a failure, of believing something God said is impossible, and of being fearful. Practice replacing those thoughts with statements of truth from the Bible.**

Chapter 3:

Make Good Decisions

We have probably all been in circumstances in which a change of mind would have done us good. Maybe we needed a new, fresh way of looking at things. Maybe we just needed an attitude adjustment. Whatever it was, God wants us to get to a place where He can work *through* us, and a renewed mind allows that to happen.

In the first couple of chapters, we dealt primarily with our thoughts, and we are going to do that again in this chapter. However, we are also going to cover some new territory; we are going to break some new ground and look at some different Bible verses concerning our will and our emotions.

Our *mind* represents the thoughts that we have. There is a constant battle going on inside of our heads, and every one of us fights this. Our *will* is our ability to choose. God has given us this incredible gift called choice. He will never override that; you always have the freedom to choose.

Working For You, Not Against You

But, if we don't think right, we are going to make bad choices, and trust me; ultimately, bad choices are going to affect you emotionally. So, all of these things work together: your mind, your choices, and your emotions/feelings; all three of these can either work together *for* you, or they can work together *against* you. They can create this perfect storm that leads to so much turmoil in our lives if we are not careful.

I want to break this down a little bit. Let's use the example of fire. Fire is a wonderful thing. It can warm you, warm your home, and cook your food. But if you don't control it and get a grip on it, it will burn your house down. It can take your life!

But, all three of these things (your mind, will, and emotions) can also work *through* and *for* you in a positive way, and what I want to show you is how. In Matthew 22:37, Jesus says:

Matthew 22:37

You shall love the Lord your God with all your heart, with all your soul and with all of your mind.

Right there are the three things we are talking about: your mind, your will, and your emotions. "With all of your heart" is referring to your emotions. "With all of your soul" is referring to your choices and decisions (your will). "With all of your mind" means your thoughts.

If there was someone in your life who loved God with every thought, choice, and emotion, what word would you use to describe that person? The word that comes to mind for me is *passion*. If you have somebody loving God with all of his or her heart, soul, and mind, I'm pretty sure that is going to be a fairly passionate person.

The point I want to make is, this is a commandment. Jesus is saying that being a passionate believer is not an option. It is a command to love God with everything, not just to occasionally dabble in Christianity. He is looking for a group of people who are *all in*.

Life is much better when you are all in with Jesus.

Ephesians chapter 6 is a very interesting passage. It deals with the whole armor of God, and the first thing Paul says is, "Take the helmet of salvation." That phrase "take the helmet" is an action phrase. That means it is not going to happen unless you take action.

God is saying, "I have provided a way for you to have good mental health. I have provided a way for you to have victory in your head, but you have got to do something with it. I have given you the helmet of salvation. Now take it, and put it on."

Isn't it interesting that we always want to put the monkey on God's back? We always want to say, "God, I don't understand. Is life ever going to be different?" And God is saying, "I have already done what I need to do. Take it, and put it on. Take what I've given you, and begin to use that."

The word *salvation* in the helmet of salvation doesn't just mean fire insurance or, "Now that I'm saved, I'm going to Heaven." It is a much broader word than that.

In fact, it is the Greek word *sozo*, which is an all-inclusive term that not only means salvation, but it also means to have peace, prosperity, good health, and a better life. Jesus Himself said this: "I've come, that you might have life and that you might have it abundantly (John 10:10)."

I always like to say I would have been satisfied if Jesus had only said, "I've come, that you might have life." But, He didn't stop there. He said, "I have come that you might have an abundant, over-the-top life." So, the word *sozo* is all of these things, all of the blessings of God and the benefits of Calvary, everything that God provided.

What He is saying is that if you don't take the helmet of salvation and put it on, the devil is going to mess with your head so much that by the time he is through with you, all you are going to have left is Heaven, not the blessings of this life until then.

Now, don't get me wrong; I'm a big fan of Heaven. But, God wants you to have joy here and to have a God-filled life. We guard that life by placing on the helmet of salvation; it is our responsibility.

I want to take a moment and try to get this into your mind. Visualize a target. This is how the enemy views your mind. He sees your mind as a target because if we think wrong, we are going to believe wrong, and every day we fight this battle with our thoughts.

The enemy is constantly bombarding our minds with all kinds of thoughts to get us to doubt God's Word or to get us to believe wrong things. In fact, the Bible says in Ephesians 6:16 that there are fiery darts. Those could be thoughts of depression, worry, inadequacy, or thoughts of the past.

All of these things are constantly and consistently attacking our minds. That is why God says to take the helmet of salvation and put it on. Why? Satan wants you to live a life of doubt and unbelief, and it *always* starts in our thinking. If we are called to be a people of faith and called to walk by faith, we have to begin to walk by faith in our thoughts.

Thoughts of F-A-I-T-H

But what does it mean to walk by faith in your thoughts? I want to take just a moment to break that down and show you how. I've taken the word *faith* and made in acrostic out of it to help you remember.

F- FOCUS

If I want to walk by faith in my thoughts, the first thing I am going to have to do is focus on the positive. This is so much more than just seeing the glass half full or half empty. I'm not just talking about having a positive attitude (although I think a positive attitude is way better than a bad attitude any day of the week).

How many people go through life, and all they focus on is the emptiness of their life? They look at their life and see all of the things that they *don't* have and that they *could* have, or all the things they are missing out on. And while they are so busy doing that, they are missing all of the good things going on in their lives.

Take an opportunity and look at your life, and I promise you, God is doing some great things right now. In fact, the older I get, the more I am a believer in the fact that all things work together for the good of those who love God and are called according to His purpose (Romans 8:28).

I have bought so much into that, that I know, when things go wrong or things go right, God's got it. I have come to a part of my life where I believe that whatever is going on in my life, God is going to use it. Even though at the time it may seem that it is against me, and even though it may seem like it is not going to work out for me, I know that God is going to turn it around.

Have you ever seen God take a situation and turn it completely around? We are going to learn to focus on the things that God is doing so that we don't miss the good things of God in our lives.

A- AFFIRM

One of the greatest tools of the enemy is self-doubt, which is thinking that you can't do something, that you are not able, not deserving, or that you never will be enough. You have got to come to the place where you say what God says about your life.

Romans 10:17 says, "Faith comes by hearing, and hearing by the Word of God." The literal translation says, "...by speaking the Word of God." I want you to notice that there is a tipping point between hearing the Word and speaking the Word.

If someone comes to me and says, "I believe in you," I appreciate that. If someone comes to me and says, "Listen, I'm telling you, you can do this. You've got what it takes!", I appreciate the encouragement. There is power in encouragement that you will never understand until someone comes and encourages you.

But the tipping point is when I begin to say to myself, "Hey, wait a minute; I *can* do what they say I can do! I *am* able to do what is expected of me! I *do* have the goods! I *do* have what it takes, and with God in me and working for me, I am going to conquer this circumstance!" Faith comes by hearing and hearing myself speak the Word of God over my situation. You are going to have to affirm yourself.

I- IMAGINE

If you are going to walk by faith in your thought life, you are going to have to imagine. I love the fact that Disney's designers are not called engineers; they are called *imagineers*. The idea is, whatever they can think of, they are going to make it come to life.

That is a Bible principle. Almost every leadership principle or good principle that you come across can be traced back to the Bible in some way. What the Bible says is that we are to call those things that be not as though they were (Romans 4:17).

Years ago, when I graduated from Bible school, my commencement speaker was Dr. T.L. Osborn. He was one of the greatest men of God that I've ever had the opportunity to meet, and he made a statement at our graduation that has always stuck with me.

He said, "If you can see it, you can have it. If you can see it with the eye of faith and if you can picture it, if you call those things that be not as though they were, God will begin to work to produce that in your life. God will give you a vision, and He will help you to bring that vision to pass."

Take just a moment, and instead of thinking about what could go *wrong*, start thinking about what might go *right*. Begin to imagine a better future and life for your family. Begin to think that God is going to inspire it. In the Bible, it says that He will give us the very desires of our heart (Psalm 37:4).

T- TRUST

Then, we are going to have to trust God in everything. As I said earlier, life is better when we are all in with Jesus. We can trust Him in everything. We need to come to the place where we say, "God, whether it's my marriage, my job, or my relationships, I just want you to know that I trust you in everything that I am doing and everything that I am going through."

H- HOLD ON

Last, here is the key: You've got to hold on. There is this thing called *perseverance,* and the reason this is difficult is because God's timetable isn't always our timetable. Sometimes the key to victory is just to not quit. Just don't give up. Keep hanging in there.

Our responsibility is not to know the season or when God is going to do it. Our responsibility is just to know that we've got to trust God, no matter how long it takes. I'm going to look to Him and let Him bring me through whatever it is I'm going through.

Where Do Thoughts Come From?

So here is the question: Where do thoughts come from? I mentioned that the average person has around 50,000 thoughts per day. The majority (85%) of those thoughts are negative, meaning that from the time we get up in the morning, it is an uphill climb just to stay positive in life.

Thoughts come from three different places. One is from your surroundings. Whatever you hear, whatever you see, and whatever you experience create these thoughts in your mind. We know that wherever we are, there are going to be thoughts coming our way. Advertisers on TV and everywhere else just bombard us, and we get sensory overload.

The second place that thoughts come from is Satan, from the enemy. Let me go ahead and make a theological statement that I think I'm on pretty firm ground on: Satan cannot read your mind. God is omniscient, which means He is all-knowing. But Satan is not and cannot read your mind. He can plant thoughts in your head and watch how you respond to those things, but Satan does not know your thoughts. He just reads your actions.

But remember, one of the places that thoughts come from is those fiery darts. Satan targets our minds with negativity, fear, and unbelief. So, what we think is a battleground for spiritual warfare.

The third place that thoughts come from is God. Earlier, we talked about how sometimes you may be sitting in church, in a worship service, and all of a sudden you have the most perverted, weird, out-there thought, and you're thinking, *where did that come from? I wasn't even thinking about that*! That is a spiritual attack to draw you out.

You might ask, "Well, what can I do to stop that from happening?" As I mentioned, you can't do anything to prevent it; you can only deal with it when it comes and manage it.

But on the other side, we have all had these God-thoughts, or times when God has spoken to our hearts words of encouragement. Or maybe God, by the Holy Spirit, has brought something back to your remembrance. Maybe it was a sermon or song, or Scripture that He used to inspire you, challenge you, or draw you more into His presence.

As we focus on the mind, understand that there is a very real battle being fought, or waged, in your head. Remember, you have *got* to bring your thoughts under the subjection, or filter, of Philippians 4:8. "Whatever things are honest, true, just, pure, lovely, or of good report, think on these things."

Your Will

Now I'd like to talk to you about the will, or you ability to choose. There is this incredible gift that God has given us called the power of choice. The will is basically *what I want, when I want it, the way I want it*, or my ability to choose.

As an illustration, imagine a cross. The cross means so many things to so many people, and I want to give you another insight into what the cross could represent.

The cross has two pieces of wood, one vertical and one horizontal. This represents our relationship with God and our relationship with other people. I've got a relationship with God, which is the vertical piece. It is when I'm talking to my heavenly Father. The horizontal beam is where I do life. That is life on Earth and people I interact with on a regular basis, my everyday life. Those are things happening all around me.

When my will intersects with God's will, I've come to a place where I have to make a decision. Am I going to do *my* will, or am I going to do God's will? That is why Jesus taught in the Lord's Prayer, "Our Father, which art in Heaven, hallowed be your name. Thy kingdom come. Thy will be done (Matthew 6:9-10)."

Whenever I have to make a decision or a choice and my will intersects God's will, I have to pray this prayer: "God, it's not what *I* want, but ultimately, what do *you* want?" And that is when I submit to the Lordship of Jesus Christ. Jesus isn't just my Savior; He is my Lord. That means He is the main decision-maker in my life. So I pray, "God, what is it that *you* want me to do?"

Let me give you a biblical example of a choice. In Deuteronomy chapter 30, Joshua says:

Deuteronomy 30:19

I call heaven and earth as witnesses today against you that I have set before you life and death, blessing and cursing. Therefore, choose life that both you and your descendants may live.

Here is what I think God is saying: I think today is a good day to make a right choice. I think today is a good day to make the decision that you have been putting off. So many times, we deal with procrastination. We say we are going to do better, make better decisions, and we are going to follow the plan of God for our life. But Joshua says here, "I am calling Heaven and Earth as witnesses *today*, that you choose life. Make that right decision."

Here is some pastoral advice: Any time you need to make a decision, you need to go to church. I think church is a place where good decisions are made. Church staff members work all week planning to provide an environment that enables you to lift the lid spiritually and experience God. They don't want anything to hinder you when you come to hear from God.

You can hear God in church. There is no way I would make a major decision in my life without first sitting in the presence of God, worshipping Him, and listening to the Holy Spirit.

So, Joshua says, "Make that choice today. I set before you life and death, blessing and cursing." And then he gives the answer. "Go ahead and choose life. It's not complicated, but so you don't miss it, go ahead and choose life."

Notice the end of that verse, "...that both you and your descendants may live." The reason that stood out to me and I wanted to share it with you is that we never make a decision that just affects us alone. When we make a decision, often it is going to affect our family and the people around us. It may affect the people we go to church with, the people we work with, and other people we regularly interact with.

Rarely do we make a decision that affects us alone. But, there are times when we make choices, and they may not stop *us*, but they may go down a generation. They may affect our children. Making decisions is a very important process.

Making Good Decisions

Therefore, I want to give you some basic ideas for what to consider before making a decision. If you are getting ready to make a big choice, I want you to ask yourself these things:

Will this decision violate the Bible?

The Bible is our rule book. It is our game book. The Bible is how we do life, and it is God's will. If I am making a decision, I want to know, *is it going to violate something that God has already told me not to do?* I want to come to the place where the Word of God is what rules my life.

Will it honor God?

What I'm about to do, is this something that is going to bring honor to God, or is it going to dishonor Him? Sometimes decisions may turn out to be neutral in this regard, but make sure you stop and ask the question beforehand, will it honor Him?

Will it make another person stumble?

I am big on grace. I'm a grace preacher and have been criticized for preaching grace, but it is in the Bible from Genesis to Revelation. God is a grace-filled God. You will never appreciate grace until you have stood in line for it.

However, even though I believe in grace and Christian liberty (whom the Son sets free is free indeed- John 8:36), I also have to come to the realization that I don't want to do anything that makes somebody around me stumble or that pushes him or her away from God.

You say, "Pastor, well that's *their* problem." Ultimately, it is their decision, but the Bible teaches that we have a responsibility to help others serve God, as well. So, I'm going to ask myself this question: What I'm going to do, even though I may have the liberty to do it, is it the heart of God? Is it really putting my brother in front of myself?

Am I really doing the right thing?

Be honest with yourself. You know deep down if what you are doing is the *right* thing or not. God's moral code has been put into us. You know if something is right or wrong, and if you are not sure, ask God to help you.

Emotions

And then there are emotions, how to deal with how you feel. Our emotions were never meant to be a guide in life. Don't ever make decisions because of how you *feel*.

Your emotions were only meant to be a gauge, just like you have a dashboard in your car. In a car, you have all of these different gauges that are telling you if things are working properly, like whether the car is running too hot, too cold, if the oil pressure is at the right place, and if the RPM's are running at the right levels.

As long as everything is right, you are doing well. But if those gauges begin to peak, you realize you've got a problem, and if you don't pull over and fix or deal with the problem, you will have a breakdown right there.

Our emotions were never meant to be a guide for our lives. I have a friend who just bought a new car. He was driving along, and he had only had the car for a couple of weeks. But, there was a light that kept coming up on his dashboard that said "check engine". Something was wrong with his brand new car!

It only had a couple hundred miles on it, and he thought, *how can that be?* He didn't want to ignore it, so he took it to the dealership. They hooked it up and did an analysis of what was going on.

They came back and said, "Here's the deal: There is nothing wrong with your car. It just has a faulty switch on the check engine light." And he said, "My car was lying to me! My car was causing me worry. It was trying to tell me something was wrong when it wasn't."

Our emotions do that all the time. They always try to tell us the wrong thing or pull us out of the Word. You cannot trust emotions as a guide for your life.

In the next chapter, we will talk about how to deal with worry and fear, how to deal with anxiety, and how to manage all of those different emotions we have, so that we can continue to move forward with God.

But, I wanted to discuss them here in the context of how our thoughts, will, and emotions work together. Remember, they can work together *for* you or *against* you. Always consider all three together, running them through the filter of God's Word, when making decisions.

ACTION STEPS

1) **List out the good things God is doing in your life, and thank Him for those things.**

2) **If you have a big decision to make, go to church and pray about it. Then, ask yourself the four questions for decision-making listed in this chapter.**

Chapter 4

Control Emotions and Choose Happiness

S o far, we have primarily dealt with our thoughts and our choices. I really can't think of any two things together that impact our lives more than those two. As I've said, if you *think* wrong, you are going to *believe* wrong, and if you *believe* wrong, you are going to *choose* wrong.

The quality of our lives is determined by the choices we make. If you make good choices, life is good. If you make bad choices, life is difficult. I once saw a meme that said, "Life is hard, but it's harder when you are stupid." So, we want to make good choices and get it right.

In this chapter, I want to go deeper into the subject of our emotions. Men, calm down. I'm not going to ask you to share your feelings. We are just going to talk about emotions, because here is the thing:

Either you will rule over your emotions, or your emotions will rule over you.

Let's begin in the book of Genesis, because there is a perfect example of someone's emotions ruling over him. In Genesis 4, we have the Adam and Eve/Cain and Abel situation. Cain and Abel were bringing their sacrifices to God. Abel did it God's way and brought the sacrifice that God required, and Cain said, "I'll just do it my way, and God will bless it."

We still do that today, right? We do things our way instead of God's way, and then we get mad at God when it doesn't work out. Cain did it his way when bringing the sacrifice. The Bible says:

Genesis 4:4-7

And Abel also brought an offering—fat portions from some of the firstborn of his flock. The Lord looked with favor on Abel and his offering, but on Cain and his offering he did not look with favor. So Cain was very angry, and his face was downcast. Then the Lord said to Cain, "Why are you angry? Why is your face downcast? If you do what is right, will you not be accepted? But if you do not do what is right, sin is crouching at your door; it desires to have you, but you must rule over it."

As a side note, your emotions affect the way you look. That's why I choose to be happy; I think it helps. When God says, "You must rule over it," He's talking about anger; that emotion is waiting right outside the door for you.

Our emotions often lead us to sin. In the book of Exodus, each of the Ten Commandments (all of the "thou shalt nots") deals with an emotion, and God is showing you how to control them.

Do not let them get out of control. Know that God is before you.

Many times, we think, "I know what God wants, but I am going to do what *I* want, and I am going to put something else first in my life." That is pride.

"Thou shalt not kill," addresses the emotion of anger, or rage. "Thou shalt not steal," addresses fear and greed (fear that I *won't* have enough and greed, thinking that I *don't* have enough).
"Thou shalt not lie," is pride again because it is when I want you to think more of me, and I don't want to be exposed in front of you. So, I'm going to tell you that I am something I am not.

Every one of the Ten Commandments deals with an emotion we have, and if we do not control our emotions, they are going to lead to sin. Emotions can rob you of peace, joy, and confidence if they get out of control. In Isaiah chapter 26, Isaiah says to God:

Isaiah 26:3

You will keep in perfect peace those whose minds are steadfast, because they trust in you.

Perfect peace doesn't come from a problem-free life. Perfect peace is not when you don't have any issues or wrinkles in life. Perfect peace comes when we keep our minds and our thoughts focused on God.

Years ago, when my wife was pregnant with our daughter, we went to one of our first doctor visits to find out if we were going to have a boy or a girl. The nurse did the ultrasound to let us know the gender, and while she was doing that, she left the room and came back with a doctor.

They went ahead and told us the gender of the baby, but the doctor said, "We have a problem. There is a mass surrounding the baby, and we don't know what it is. So, we are going to refer you to a specialist."

Right away, what was supposed to be a happy, exciting moment turned into something where we didn't know what we were facing or what the future was going to look like. We had to wait five days before we could get in to see the specialist.

Here is what we knew: For the next five days, we had to make a choice. We asked ourselves, *for the next five days, are we going to decide to be in fear, worry, and dread? Or, are we going to do everything we can to keep our minds on God and keep our peace about us?* We made the decision that we were going to focus on God, not on what was around us or what we were facing.

We had literally hundreds of opportunities to believe God in those next five days, hundreds of opportunities to trust God. When you do that, the enemy comes at you relentlessly, trying to get you to doubt what God is doing.

We went back five days later to the specialist. We were a "crisis pregnancy", and they confirmed what the doctor had said. There was something there, and they didn't know what it was. They *did* know that if we dealt with it, we could endanger the life of the baby. So, that was never a choice for us.

We decided to just go forward with the mass still there. My wife carried the baby full-term, and she is a beautiful young lady today (with a little bit of an attitude, but we're working on that).

After she was born, the mass was gone and the doctor said, "We don't know what it was, where it went, or anything like that. But she is fine, and everything is perfect!"

Do Not Worry

You are always going to have an opportunity to entertain the worst-case scenario. In fact, in the New Testament, one of my favorite stories is the story of when Jesus was in the boat with His disciples.

A storm came up, and the King James Version says that Jesus was "asleep in the bottom of the boat". Other translations say that He was "going to sleep". You might think that there is really not much of a difference there, but in reality, there is a huge difference!

In other words, Jesus was awake when the storm came. He felt the wind blowing. He felt the waves slapping the side of the boat. He felt the boat rocking, and He could hear the panic in the voices of the disciples because they thought they were going to die.

In the midst of all of that noise and the storm, Jesus still held onto His peace, to the point that He said, "I think I'll go ahead and take a nap in the midst of the storm."

That should be our story, as well. Whatever is going on, say, "I am going to have the peace of God, because I'm going to keep my mind on God." In fact, in that same story, Jesus asked his disciples, "Why are you so fearful?" And then He answered his own question. "How is it that you have no faith?" They were so fearful, because they had no faith.

When storms come, you have to choose to refuse fear.

There may be a storm in your family or a financial storm. There may be a storm in your health. Have you ever noticed that when you face a fearful situation, Satan's propaganda machine immediately goes into overdrive? He creates all of these worst-case scenario headlines about how bad things are, how they are never going to turn around, how horrible it's going to be, and how you are probably going to die. He does everything he can to get you to worry.

The best advice I can give you to combat worry is to read Psalm 91, which is what I call "God's 911". Think on that passage; meditate on it, and just let God use it to drive the fear out of your life. It is filled with promises of what God will do for the person who keeps his or her faith and eyes on Him.

Fear always leads to worry. Let me give you a couple of definitions of worry. Worry is using your imagination to create something you don't want. Another definition is that it is like walking around with an umbrella, waiting for rain.

In other words, you are just looking for something bad to happen and expecting the worst to come. It may be a beautiful day, but you choose to focus on what *could* happen, rather than on what *is* happening right in front of you.

One of the best stories I've heard about needless worry is this one: There was a small village, and early one morning the people were awoken by a crazy man running through the streets of their village, banging on the doors screaming, "Run for your life! The dam is broken!" Everybody instinctively grabbed their kids, leaving all of their possessions behind. In full panic mode, they ran out of town and out of harm's way.

There was one older gentleman who ran as far as he could to the edge of town but realized, "There is no way I am ever going to be able to escape the flood waters." He just sat down on a rock at the edge of town with all of the people running past him in panic. He turned around and looked at where the dam was, and all he saw was a beautiful sunrise and the dam completely in tact. There were no flood waters coming.

Oftentimes, we run because of something that isn't there. We run because of what we *think* might be there and because of some outward influence. There may not be any truth in it whatsoever. Make sure there is actually a problem before you start to worry, and if there really is a problem, trust God with the outcome. In Psalm 15:15, God says:

Psalm 15:15

Call on me in your day of trouble. I will answer you, and you will praise me.

I like that, because He didn't say, "I might" and "You might." He said, "I will" and "You will." We will praise Him, because He will have answered our prayers. God is a good God. There is no reason to fear.

Do you worry more than you should? Listen to what Jesus said about worry in Matthew chapter six. Jesus is teaching (He always preached the best sermons), and He said:

Matthew 6:25-32

Therefore I tell you, do not worry about your life, what you will eat or drink; or about your body, what you will wear. Is not life more than food, and the body more than clothes? Look at the birds of the air; they do not sow or reap or store away in barns, and yet your heavenly Father feeds them. Are you not much more valuable than they? Can any one of you by worrying, add a single hour to your life? And why do you worry about clothes? See how the flowers of the field grow. They do not labor or spin. Yet I tell you that not even Solomon in all his splendor was dressed like one of these. If that is how God clothes the grass of the field, which is here today and tomorrow is thrown into the fire, will he not much more clothe you— you of little faith? So do not worry, saying, 'What shall we eat?' or 'What shall we drink?' or 'What shall we wear?' For the pagans run after all these things, and your heavenly Father knows that you need them.

Here, Jesus preaches this incredible sermon about worry, and five times in these few verses, He says, "Do not worry." Five times, He says, "Do not be anxious." Five times he says, "Take no thought about it." So, He is preaching it over and over again. Don't worry; just trust.

WHY You Should Not Worry

Why should you not worry? I want to give you four reasons. These could be things that are Christian catchphrases or things you have heard before, but the point is, either these are real and true, or they aren't.

God is for you.

He is on your side. He is pulling for you. God wants you to succeed. He is not "the man upstairs"; He is your heavenly Father, and He wants to see you do well. He created you and knows what is best for you. Trust in His goodness.

He said, "I will never leave you, nor forsake you."

No matter what you go through, you are not going to face it alone. God is saying, "I will be there with you." I think it is so important that when you are facing something, you know you have a support group.

When you hear of someone in a crisis, get a hold of them and tell them, "You're not going to go through this alone. You have a family that loves you. You have a support group, people who want to be involved in your life." Make phone calls, and send out prayer videos. It's huge for people to know that they can count on you.

Jesus is the same yesterday, today, and tomorrow.

That means that whatever He has done, He will do. He never changes and can be trusted to not do anything that is outside of His nature. The Jesus you read about in the Bible is the same today as He was then and before the foundation of the world.

God can do anything but fail.

He is omnipotent, which means all-powerful. So, He is capable of anything, but failure is not in His nature; it is not a part of His character.

If you put all of those together, you have reasons for rest and confidence. You cannot worry and be happy at the same time. You have to make up your mind to say, "Am I going to choose to be happy, or am I going to worry about my circumstances?"

Major Cause of Unhappiness

Aside from worry, there are some major reasons why people are unhappy, and I would like to share them to hopefully help you avoid them.

Guilt

Guilt is one of those unseen things. Someone once described guilt as being like an invisible giant in your life. It may come because of something you said, something you did, or something that happened in the past that you have never dealt with. It is like a giant you cannot get past without divine help.

You know I like the story of David and Goliath, because I mentioned it in Chapter One. Guilt is like the giant, Goliath, and here is the thing about Goliath: No one could get around him. You couldn't sneak past him, and you couldn't ignore the fact that he was there. In other words, David knew he was going to have to deal with the giant in front of him.

You cannot just dismiss guilt. Somewhere down the road, you are going to have to deal with it. If you don't face it, it will eat you up inside. But how do you face the giant of guilt? You do it with grace, through the cross of Jesus Christ.

If you do not understand grace, you will never have the peace of God. If you do not understand that God has forgiven you (not because of who *you* are, but because of who *Jesus* is), if you do not understand that God sees you as perfect through Jesus, then you will never understand the blessings of God. You will never walk in the freedom or peace of God that He wants you to have. It always comes through faith.

Anger

Another major cause of unhappiness is anger. In life, you can choose if you are going to be bitter or if you are going to be better. There are a lot of angry people walking around, and here are some things that anger does to your body medically: It produces insomnia, heart attacks, headaches, alcoholism, and ulcers. It is never a good choice to hold onto anger in your life. You need to forgive as Jesus forgave you in order to find freedom.

Selfishness

I have often said that in every marriage relationship, if there is tension and discord, someone is being selfish in your marriage. Somebody in the marriage has said, "I want what *I* want, and I am going to do things *my* way; this is what *I* want to happen." Someone has put himself or herself in front of the spouse. God says you are there to *serve* your spouse, and selfishness will ultimately make you unhappy.

Unresolved Conflict

Jesus made this statement: "Blessed are the peacemakers." He did not say those who want peace or would just like to have peace, but those who *make* peace. A peacemaker is someone who actively seeks to resolve conflict.

There is a door in Dublin, Ireland, in St. Patrick's Cathedral called the Door of Reconciliation, which was used in the 1400's. There were two families who were fighting against each other. Right outside of the castle walls and courtyard, these two families, the Butlers and the FitzGeralds had been in a long-term feud. It broke out into a full war, and several on each side were killed.

The Butlers retreated into the church, and there they claimed sanctuary, which meant if they were inside the walls of the church, they were safe. No one could come in, because they were under the protection of the church.

So, the FitzGeralds came to the door and began to bang on it. There was a long argument that we are told went on for hours; both sides were screaming and yelling at each other.

Finally after a while, when everyone had cooled down, one of the men from the FitzGeralds (Gerald FitzGerald), on the outside of the church, invited the Butlers to come out.

They said, "No way! If we come out, you are going to kill us."
The FitzGeralds said, "No, we are not going to kill you. Let's bring this thing to an end."
But the Butlers responded, "No, we are not coming out."

So, Gerald took a battle axe and chopped a hole in the door of the church. He stuck his arm through that hole, extending it as a gesture of friendship and forgiveness.

Think about the faith and courage that took! When he stuck his arm through that door, a lot of things could have happened. They could have broken his arm. They could have grabbed it and held him captive. They could have cut his arm off. But, as a gesture, he extended his hand through the door to say, "This is my word. Let's make this thing right. Let's stop it here." Thus, we have the Door of Reconciliation. They have it on display in St. Patrick's Cathedral in Dublin.[4]

Blessed are the peacemakers. Blessed are those who take action. Blessed are those who work toward peace.

Here is the question: Why should I care about conflict? Let me tell you why. If I am living a life of conflict, it blocks my relationship with God. In fact, here is how important it is:

God said that if you have conflict and then come to church to worship, but you have not dealt with the conflict, don't even bother worshipping. If you bring a gift to the altar and you have conflict and strife in your life, go fix all of that strife; then come and worship (Matthew 5:24). We have to realize how bad strife is and what it does.

It also cuts you off in prayer; it hinders your prayer life, especially conflict in a marriage relationship. In 1 Peter 3:7, it says that if a husband and wife are not in agreement, their prayers are not going to be answered.

Conflict hinders your happiness. Psalm 118:24 says, "This is the day that the Lord has made. I will rejoice and be glad in it." You can choose to rejoice and have an attitude of thankfulness.

Truths About Your Attitude

I will conclude this chapter with two truths about your attitude, because your attitude is directly related to happiness. First, your attitude is always your choice. We cannot control what happens around us; we can only control how we respond to it.

For example, you cannot change the past if you have experienced the death of a loved one. You might not be able to see how you can go forward when someone in your life has died, whether it is a child or pregnancy that went wrong or perhaps a parent. And you look at your life thinking, *I don't think I can ever be happy again, because that person who meant so much to me is no longer in my life.* You have made the choice to continue to mourn.

You cannot change the fact that someone you love has died. The only thing you can do is what David did in 2 Samuel 12:22.

When David's son died, he mourned, and then he said, "I can't bring him back. No matter how long I cry, no matter how much I long for it, I cannot bring my son back. But, I can go and be with him. Therefore, I am going to live my life. In this short span I have, I will live, and I know that when I die, I can be united with my loved one again."

Also, you cannot change the decisions that your grown kids make. You may be heartbroken because of things they have done and the choices they have made. You can't change that, but you can keep praying for them, loving them, supporting them, and sharing God with them. You can do all that you know to do, but you are no longer responsible after a certain age.

The second truth about your attitude that I would like to share is that an attitude of gratitude produces miracles. Take a moment and look at people who are living unhappy, negative, and critical lives. Their own attitude is holding them hostage. Your attitude either attracts people to you, or it pushes people away from you.

If you say, "I don't know why no one in my family likes me," it could be you. Rick Warren once said (concerning attitude), "Sometimes God is more interested in changing your attitude than your circumstances."[5]

So, I want to encourage you to choose joy. Of all the emotions out there, I want you to choose joy. You won't *feel* it first; you have to *choose* it first.

Choices lead, and feelings follow.

In 2 Corinthians 6:10, Paul is writing, and this is an incredible, positive verse. He is talking about all of the difficulties going on, and he says, "I am sorrowful, yet always rejoicing." That word *yet* is a powerful word. He said, "I am poor, yet I am making many rich. I have nothing, yet I possess everything."

In every situation Paul found himself in, he said, "I choose joy. I choose to see the positive side. I choose to see the best in life. Philippians 4:4 says, "Rejoice in the Lord always, and again I say rejoice!" Some of you have not "joiced" for the first time, but REjoice means you have got to do it again. You have to continually choose to have joy in your life.

In this chapter, we tackled the topics of our emotions, overcoming worry, and choosing happiness and joy. In the last chapter, we will revisit where we started, and I will give some additional advice for moving our minds from where they are to where they need to be, so you can stop getting stuck in negative, harmful thought patterns.

ACTION STEPS

1) **If you are in a storm in your life, decide today to keep your eyes on God and be at peace, rather than deciding to be full of fear and dread.**

2) **Read Psalm 91, and meditate on it.**

Chapter 5

Focus and Grow

T his whole time, we have really been talking about getting our heads in the right frame of mind. I want to begin this chapter by backing up a little bit and going over some of the highlights, so we can fit everything together.

Review

I mentioned in the first chapter, and I want to repeat, that if you know of anyone struggling with depression, struggling through life, struggling with thoughts or signs of suicide, please reach out to them. And if *you* are having those thoughts, please reach out for help. Let me help you. There are numbers to call. There are people who will pray with you, and there are other areas where we can get you help. It is so important that you do that.

Suicide is a permanent answer to a temporary problem. We *can* fix what you are going through. Again, if you know of someone who may be struggling in that area, go to them, be a friend, and support them.

Remember, a lot of people who are considering suicide and are struggling are doing so because of depression. There are two major causes of depression. One is faulty thinking (which has really been the heart of this book).

And the other cause, which ultimately leads to self-harm, is isolation. Those are two of the greatest tools that Satan uses against us. He uses wrong thinking and then separates us from other people who could be helpful in our lives.

Remember, if your voice is the only voice you are listening to as you are going through life, you are already in trouble. We need other people. And I will just be bold and tell you, you need a pastor. You need someone who is speaking into your life and is hearing God *with* you. He is not the only source, but he is hearing God for you and with you. You need people in your life who can talk to you and give you counsel.

The Bible says there is wisdom in a multitude of counsel (Proverbs 15:22). You need a lot of people who are speaking into your life, and I encourage you to get involved with others in some way. The enemy loves to isolate you, and that is why it is so important to get connected in a small group. In small groups, we hear other voices and have other people to help us up.

Another one of the major thoughts from the first chapter that I want to repeat is the illustration of changing the channel. If you are ever sitting at home watching a really bad program, you do not have to sit there and endure it. You can change the channel. If you are watching a program that has a certain cringe factor to it, you just don't like it, or it is giving you bad vibrations, you can just simply change the channel.

How foolish would it be to sit there and continue to watch something that you do not like? Have you ever walked out on a movie? There are certain thoughts that you need to walk out on. You need to close the door on those things and how you do that is through what I call "repent and replace".

Repent means to go another direction, but it also means to change your mind. If you are thinking negative, self-defeating, broken thoughts, you need to tell God you are sorry, because your mind is not lining up with His Word, and you are not doing what it says, not running things through the filter of Philippians 4:8 ("Whatever is true, noble, right, pure, lovely, admirable, if anything is excellent or of good report, think about such things").

We need to say, "God, I repent and change my mind." We replace that with, "I can do all things through Christ, who strengthens me (Philippians 4:13)."
"I am God's workmanship (Ephesians 2:10)."
"I am valuable to God; I am the apple of His eye (Psalm 17:8)."

The only thing stronger than a thought is a word, and in order to defeat a negative thought, you need to speak a word to overcome it. That is a very powerful principle. We replace whatever we are struggling with, with a Scripture verse and find a way to think on that instead.

In the last chapter, we talked about our emotions. Let me just say this: Your emotions, left unchecked, will lead to sin. We talked about how each of the Ten Commandments deals with an emotion. Every one of the Commandments is saying, "Don't let this emotion take over your life."

Focus

As we wrap up, I want to give a few more things that could be helpful to you. I don't know if you are a nature lover or an ornithologist (someone who studies birds), but there is a bird called a cuckoo bird (No, it is not cuckoo for Cocoa Puffs).

Something that is interesting about this bird is, this is what scientists call a *brood parasite*. This bird has a certain tendency to lay its eggs in the nests of other birds. Then, it relies on the other mother birds to raise its chicklings.

Because this bird is bigger than most other birds, when the baby cuckoo hatches out, it is bigger than the other baby birds in the nest. So, one of two things happens.

Because it is bigger and needs more room, it will usually kick the other birds out of the nest, and they are left to die. If that doesn't happen, when the mother bird begins to feed the baby birds (again because the baby cuckoo is bigger), when she shows up with food, all she sees is a gigantic head and this really huge mouth. She ends up feeding the cuckoo bird, while all of the other baby birds die out.

You might be connecting the dots and seeing that when something gets planted in our minds and we begin to focus on that, it is going to push out every other thought. And one of the things I have said is that your life always goes in the direction of your strongest thought.

Whatever you spend the most time focusing on and dwelling on is the direction you will go. Once a thought is planted and you begin to feed it, it becomes bigger and bigger. But here's the takeaway:

Feed the thoughts that you want to see grow.

For some people, you just need to stop dwelling on bad things that have happened in your life. You can't change them. Stop thinking about that ex-boyfriend or girlfriend. Stop thinking about how badly your ex mistreated you. Stop thinking about all of the negative things that have happened in your life. Stop digging up all of that hurt and focusing on it, unless that is the direction you want your life to go.

I want to share with you a couple of Scripture verses, beginning with Psalm 1:

Psalm 1:1-2

Blessed is the one who does not walk in step with the wicked or stand in the way that sinners take or sit in the company of mockers, but whose delight is in the law of the Lord, and who meditates on his law day and night.

Let's take this verse and break it down from walking to standing to sitting, until we get to this word *meditating* and what this word really means. Let's see what God's Word says about walking, standing, and sitting in this context.

Who are you walking with? Amos 3:3 says it is hard for two people to walk together unless they be agreed. So, with whom are you walking? The Bible clearly says that bad company corrupts good morals (1 Corinthians 15:33). You are who you hang out with. The people you surround yourself with really do impact your life.

I want to encourage you to surround yourself with people who will lift you up. Surround yourself with people who can encourage you, stretch you, grow you, and speak positive, life-giving things into your life.

And, you need to make a separation from the other people who are dragging you down. It doesn't mean that you don't love them or care for them anymore. You just need to realize that there has to be a separation, or you will end up in the same situation they are in.

You are who you hang out with.

I mentioned loneliness earlier, and when I say that, I don't mean to just stop right where you are and avoid everybody. Satan loves to isolate us, and bad things happen when we are isolated. The first thing God said when He created man was. "It is not good that man should be alone (Genesis 2:18)." He was saying, "I don't want you to be lonely, so I am going to create people for you to be with."

We need each other. We need small groups. We need people in our lives who, when we are down, will lift us. When we are hurting, they can comfort us. Or, there may be times when *you* are the lifter and encourager. Those are the things that God has called you to do. Ecclesiastes 4:10 says, "Woe to him that is alone, because when he falls, he has no one to pick him up." Don't live a lonely, isolated life.

Now, this is just from a pastor's viewpoint, and it's some free advice. Over my years of pastoring, I've noticed that when people get lonely, they do really stupid things and make really stupid decisions. They get in bad relationships and get themselves into terrible situations.

So, God knew exactly what He was talking about when He said in Genesis 2:18, "It is not good for man to be alone." We are not at our best when we are alone. But, we need the *right* people in our lives.

Back to Psalm 1. Don't walk with that person who drags you down. Instead, stand. Stand means to *take a stand*, to choose. You really need to know what it is that you believe. This verse is talking about making choices. Choose where you are on an issue, and get some convictions in your life.

Find out what you believe, and then believe your beliefs.

A number of years ago, God spoke with me and impressed something upon my heart. It was one of those times when I said, "Ouch, God!" It was unexpected, and what He said hurt.

But God spoke to me and said, "I want you to begin to believe what you say you believe." It's one thing to have knowledge in your head, but it is another thing when it becomes a part of your heart. So, know what you are standing on and standing for. Make right choices. We spent a whole chapter talking about that.

Finally, the word *sit* in Psalm 1 is painting a picture of a person who has come to a place where all they do now is sit and criticize and complain. Either you are part of the solution, or you are part of the problem. Don't become that person who becomes constantly critical and cynical about life or about everything around you.

Deuteronomy 11:18 says, "Fix these words of mine in your hearts and minds; tie them as symbols on your hands, and bind them on your foreheads." Again, he is talking about that word *meditate* that we mentioned in Chapter Two.

Remember, meditation is not a New Age thing; it is a Bible thing. We need to sit and focus our thoughts on God. Take time to let God's Word get from your head to your heart.

What meditation does is, it takes the Word of God that you are hearing or reading, takes it off of the page, and puts it deep down into your spirit, where it becomes a belief. It is one thing to say that you *know* something and another thing to *believe* something. To meditate on the Word of God means to speak God's Word yourself or to practice it regularly. Meditation pushes God's Word down into your life until it becomes a habit, or becomes established.

We have to learn to develop these thought habits. A habit is something you do over and over again until it becomes a part of you, and your mind is such an incredible machine and gift from God, that once you start doing something, if you do it three, four, or half a dozen times, your mind will say, "I've got it. Don't even think about it anymore." And your mind goes on autopilot so you don't have to use that energy. It just runs that part of your life through certain triggers.

We can learn to develop thought habits such that we automatically begin to think in a *good* way or in a right direction. As you meditate on God's Word, it permanently attaches itself to your soul.

Deuteronomy 11 says to "bind the Word on your forehead". The Hasidic Jews (very traditional Jews) from Bible times and still today, take Scripture passages, write them down, and put them in boxes called tefillin. Then, they tie the boxes around their foreheads, literally fulfilling the command. This just shows how serious they were, and still are, about God's Word.

We don't do this in our culture, but we do need to start each day with a biblical thought. Every morning, I start my day with a quick devotion, about a page and a half. I read it and always have a positive thought for the day. I begin to focus on that thought, and five or six times a day, I find myself going back to that verse or thought and thinking on it. The more I think about it, the more things God brings to me to enlarge that thought in my life.

Transitioning the Mind

Now that we know what kind of thought habits we need to develop in order to grow and move forward, I'd like to again reinforce the idea of change, or transition, and see what that looks like. There are three distinct ways in which our minds should move *from* one thing *to* another.

Move from being undisciplined to becoming disciplined in your thoughts.

The best example that I know to use of an undisciplined mind is that of an unruly three-year-old. Have you ever been in a restaurant, on a plane, or somewhere where someone had a child who was totally out of control? He or she was jumping on things, running around, or screaming. I'm sure that is not an enjoyable experience.

When that happens, you think to yourself, *where is the parent? Who is in charge here?* Obviously the child is. But, we all know that it is not the three-year-old's fault. If we could get away with it, we would behave that way, too. You look around and think, *there has got to be a parent around somewhere who is in charge.*

When you don't rule over your mind or reel it in, it will go wild just like that child. You are the parent in charge of the thoughts you have. And if you just let your mind go in every direction and think on everything like fear, worry, and problems, you are being undisciplined in your thinking. You need to discipline your thoughts.

That is why the Bible says, "Bring every thought captive and subjected to the lordship of Jesus Christ (2 Corinthians 10:5)." Ask yourself, "Is this something I need to think on?" Remember the Philippians 4:8 filter again. Think on the things that are true, noble, right, pure..." It is your responsibility to reel your mind in and not have it going in every direction.

Move from a confused mind to an established mind.

There are a lot of people with a lot of confusion in their heads. One of the things I have discovered is that often, confusion comes from the enemy. The Bible says that God is not the author of confusion.

Sometimes, when we are confused about things that are going on, it can be a spiritual attack, and Satan is trying to defeat you in the arena of your head. In these cases, we need to move from being confused to being established. That is when you truly believe your beliefs.

Someone who lives in confusion is what the Bible calls a *double-minded* person. In the book of James, it says that whoever is double-minded will not receive anything from God, because that person is on-again/off-again (James 1:7-8). He was going one way and then changed his mind to go the other way. God wants us to move out of confusion to the place where we establish our thoughts. The only way we can do that is to know what it is that we really believe.

You have got to nail those things down until they become convictions in your life. Sometimes when you are in a state of confusion, you just need to pick *something*. I'm not talking about evil over good or something that is sinful. But sometimes, if you are not sure, just make a choice.

Just do something to get your life off of high center. One of the things I've said so many times is that it is difficult to steer a parked car. But, once you start moving, it is a lot easier to turn that thing around and get it going in the right direction.

The Bible says that the steps of a righteous man or a righteous woman are ordered of the Lord (Psalm 37:23). If you are going in the wrong direction, God has a way of turning you around and getting you back on track. But you've got to make a choice and choose to get out of that confusion you are in. So, move from being confused to becoming established.

Move from having a wounded mind to having a healed mind.

There are a lot of people who are wounded in their thoughts and their emotions and have never brought those things to God for healing. A wound left untreated never gets better. It always gets worse.

If you don't bring it to God for healing or for Him to do a work in your life, you are never going to get past your past. You are never going to be able to move forward and let God do something different in your life. Psalm 31:10 says:

Psalm 31:10

My life is consumed by anguish and my years by groaning; my strength fails because of my affliction, and my bones grow weak.

But, the Bible also says that a merry heart does good, like medicine (Proverbs 17:22). Remember, you can choose joy, and when you do, God says that is like medicine for your life and for your soul.

A merry heart does good, like medicine, but a person with a wounded heart, the Bible says, is like a city with broken down walls (Proverbs 25:28). In Bible days, the walls around a city were its protection. The stronger the walls were, the safer the people behind the walls were.

But, if those walls were broken down or torn down, that meant the enemy could come in and out at will and wreak whatever havoc it wanted on that city.

So, if you have a wounded spirit and you are not letting God heal it, it simply means the enemy has total access into your life and is going to continue to keep that part of your life stirred up. I want you to take that wound and present it to God for healing.

There are a lot of young people cutting themselves. In fact, there are so many, they have been given the name "cutters". These are young people who are so emotionally disturbed on the inside, that it affects them on the outside, and they cut themselves. They are hurting so badly and have so much pain and anguish on the inside, that they are acting on the outside, cutting themselves, and making the situation worse.

Well, we also have spiritual cutters. These are people who won't deal with the issues and let God heal them. All it does is continue to put them on this downward slope in their walk with God. You can bring it to God for healing. He cares. He wants to heal that area of your life. God wants to heal your brokenness.

Move from religion to grace.

There are people who have a religious mindset, and God wants us to have a grace mindset.

Jesus did not come to Earth to establish a religion. Jesus came so we could have a *relationship* with God.

There is this thing called sin that separated us from God. Jesus became the bridge between God and man, so that we could walk together and again have interaction with God. So, all that we do in Christianity is not about promoting a religion; it is about a relationship with Jesus. It is about restoring that relationship with God.

The only way we can do that is when we first receive God's grace into our lives. We cannot keep all of the rules and regulations to live a perfect life. We need grace. But even after we find that grace, we need to get rid of our religious mindset.

If we are not careful, we begin to put everybody in a box and say, "You need to line up with me. You need to act the way that I act and think the way that I think." We begin to judge people because they are not behaving the way that we think they should behave.

We need to give people grace. Maybe you are different from me. Maybe you act differently and do things differently, but I still love you. We are not called to be the Holy Spirit in the lives of others; we are called to be God's good news in the lives of others.

That means you don't have to judge or correct everybody. You can just be the person who shows them the love of God, and then let God change them. Think about this: The Holy Spirit did just fine without you before you came along. And long after you are gone, He will still be very successful at bringing people to Christ, because that is what He does.

However, He gives us the profound privilege of participating in bringing people to Him. Let's do that with love and grace.

A Life Verse

I want to leave you with one last verse. This is a verse that would be a great life verse, and it is Colossians 2:7.

Colossians 2:7

Being rooted and built up in Him, strengthened in the faith as you were taught, and overflowing with thankfulness.

The words *rooted* and *built up* are so important. First of all, God wants you to grow, and He wants you to grow up. In order to do that, He has got to get you established in the things of Him. A tree can only grow as high as its root system will allow it. If it doesn't have good and strong roots, the first storm that comes along is going to blow it over.

So, the roots determine how far and how deep we can go with God. What you are doing when you go to church and listen to biblical teachings is, you are establishing your root system. God wants to grow you and build you up, but He has got to first get your feet established.

As a pastor, I am not called to inspire you. Some people say, "I want you to be more inspirational." Trust me; I do too, but it is not my gift. I am not called to inspire you; I am called to *ground* you. I am called to root you, be an anchor, and to establish you so that you can begin to grow.

I am just meat and potatoes. I give you all of things you need to establish yourself in the things of God, so God can grow you up in Him, strengthen you in the faith, and allow you to overflow with thankfulness. That is the life that God wants you to have.

ACTION STEPS

1) Consider who you hang out with the most. Do those people encourage you or drag you down? If they drag you down, consider separating yourself from them.

2) Get in the habit of starting your day with a Bible verse or passage. Think about it throughout the day to keep your mind on track.

Conclusion

All of these things we have discussed about renewing your mind and changing the way you think are for the purpose of setting you on a path of being mentally stable, as well as mentally and spiritually strong.

1) Chapter One was all about identifying those thoughts that are holding you back, harming you, and leaving you stuck. We need to establish that filter for our thoughts from Philippians 4:8, repent, and choose to change the channel, so to speak.

2) In Chapter Two, we talked about replacing damaging thoughts with biblical ones. Speak God's Word over your life, and dwell on that instead. Also, find a good pastor to walk with you and give you guidance. None of us can do life alone.

3) In Chapter Three, we looked at an acrostic for the word FAITH to see what it looks like to walk by faith and trust in God's goodness. We also talked about the gift of free will and questions to ask to help us make good decisions that are right and that honor God.

4) Chapter Four was all about our emotions and why we should not worry. Remember, if you do not rule over your emotions, they will rule over you. Choose not to let fear and anger drive your life. Choose to trust God because He will never fail you, and choose an attitude of thankfulness and joy.

5) Finally, in Chapter Five, we reviewed how Satan tries to trap and isolate us, but also how, if we focus on God's Word, we can develop strong roots, grow in the Lord, and live in victory.

I hope this book has given you some helpful guidance and advice for "changing your mind". If someone you know is struggling with depression or thoughts of suicide, if you need help applying these principles to your life, or if you desire to have a relationship with Jesus, please contact us at Cornerstone Church. We are here to help you.

Cornerstone Church
9900 SE 15th
Midwest City, OK 73130
Phone: 405-737-5599
https://www.cornerstone.tv/
https://www.ronmckey.com/

References

[1]*National Geographic*, "Human Brain: Facts and Information." October 2009. https://www.nationalgeographic.com/science/he alth-and-human-body/human-body/brain/

[2]Stone, Miller, and Molina. "Pastor and Mental Health Advocate Dies by Suicide": *Christianity Today International.* September 2019. https://www.christianitytoday.com/news/2019/se ptember/pastor-mental-health-advocate-jarrid-wilson-dies-sui- cide.html

[3]Peale, Norman Vincent. *The Power of the Plus Factor*. Fleming H. Revell Company, 1987.

[4]"The Door of Reconciliation". May 2016. https://www.stpatrickscathedral.ie/the-door-of-re conciliation/

[5]Warren, Rick. "Your Life is Shaped by Your Thoughts", Pastor Rick.com. August 2018. https://pastorrick.com/devotional/english/your-life-is-shaped-by- your-thoughts4

The Holy Bible: King James Version.

The Holy Bible: New International Version

About the Author

Being pastors is more than a career choice for Ron and Carol McKey; it is a calling burning deep inside. It drives them to stay creative and relevant in communicating the life-changing message of Jesus Christ in an ever-changing culture that needs to see, hear, and feel the love of God.

With over 35 years of experience pastoring children, youth, and adults, they have remained true to their purpose of reaching the entire family. Pastor Ron McKey communicates in a way that speaks to today's culture, focusing on how to apply Christ's teachings to our lives, so we can experience God's incredible purpose each and every day.

https://www.ronmckey.com/

www.ingramcontent.com/pod-product-compliance
Lightning Source LLC
Chambersburg PA
CBHW031629040426
42452CB00007B/745